EXAMINING POETRY

A practical guide for 15—18 year olds

MICHAEL AND PETER BENTON

HODDER AND STOUGHTON

LONDON SYDNEY AUCKLAND TORONTO

British Library Cataloguing in Publication Data

Benton, Michael
   Examining poetry: a practical guide for
   15–18 year olds.
   1. English poetry—History and criticism
   2. Criticism
   I. Title   II. Benton, Peter
   821'.009   PR504.5

ISBN 0 340 32572 0

First published 1986
Third impression 1987

Printed in Great Britain
for Hodder and Stoughton Educational
a division of Hodder and Stoughton Ltd, Mill Road
Dunton Green, Sevenoaks, Kent by
St Edmundsbury Press Limited, Bury St Edmunds, Suffolk

Contents

Acknowledgements

For permission to quote copyright material the authors and publishers wish to thank the following: 'Mary, Mary Magdalene' from *Collected Poems* by Charles Causley, reprinted by permission of Macmillan; 'Esther's Tomcat' from *Lupercal*, 'The Jaguar' from *The Hawk in the Rain* and 'The Warm and the Cold' from *Season Songs* all by Ted Hughes, reprinted by permission of Faber and Faber Ltd (permission for 'The Jaguar' is also given by Harper & Row, Publishers, Inc.): 'Ambulances' from *The Whitsun Weddings* by Philip Larkin, reprinted by permission from Faber and Faber Ltd; 'In a Station of the Metro' from *Collected Shorter Poems* by Ezra Pound, reprinted by permission from Faber and Faber Ltd; 'Born Yesterday' from *The Less Deceived* by Philip Larkin, reprinted by permission from The Marvell Press; 'Cock-Crow' from *Collected Poems* by Edward Thomas, reprinted by permission from Mrs Myfanway Thomas and Faber and Faber Ltd; 'Metaphors' and 'Mirror' from *Collected Poems* by Sylvia Plath (Faber and Faber Ltd), © 1967 and 1971 Ted Hughes; 'Poplar' from *The Candy-floss Tree* poems by Gerda Mayer, Frank Flynn and Norman Nicholson (1984), © Gerda Mayer 1984, reprinted by permission of Oxford University Press; 'The Pond' from *The Stones of Emptiness* by Anthony Thwaite, reprinted by permission of Anthony Thwaite and Oxford University Press; 'The Fat Black Woman Goes Shopping' from *The Fat Black Woman's Poems* by Grace Nichols, reprinted by permission of Virago Press Limited, © Grace Nichols 1984; 'The Tom-Cat' from *Poems and Portraits by Don Marquis*, © Sun Printing and Publishing Assoc., reprinted by permission of Doubleday & Company, Inc.; 'Why I Gave you the Chinese Plate' from *Dreaming Frankenstein and Collected Poems* by Liz Lochhead, reprinted by permission of Polygon Books; 'Nothing Gold Can Stay' and 'Spring Pools' from *The Poetry of Robert Frost* edited by Edward Connery Lathem, reprinted by permission of Jonathan Cape and Holt, Rinehart and Winston; 'Dissection' by Colin Rowbotham, reprinted by permission of Colin Rowbotham; 'A Negro Woman' from *Pictures from Breughel* by William Carlos Williams, © 1955 William Carlos Williams, reprinted by permission of New Directions Publishing Corporation; for examination questions: Associated Examination Board, University of Cambridge Examination Board, Southern Regional Examinations Board and The Northern Examining Association.

Introduction

Your poetry lessons in school so far will probably have been spent in reading and talking about a variety of poems; you may have 'performed' some aloud, recorded some on tape or made your own anthologies. You will probably have written some of your own poems, too, and may have contributed to wall displays or a duplicated magazine. The purpose of this short book is to build on this foundation and to help you develop the skills of reading and writing about poems so that you can both enjoy these activities and approach examination work with confidence.

One important thing to realise is that varied reading, informal chat and creative writing are all ways of enjoying and learning about poetry. Above all, your personal responses to a poem remain vital. This book aims to help you to respond to poetry through close reading and precise writing and to sharpen your critical faculties through the activities it offers. It is not a course, not a solution to the examination problem; but we hope the workbook approach will give you experience in handling poems so that you can cope with the demands of formal written work on your own. The book is designed to help you whether you are working as an individual student or as a member of a class.

Poetry should be a regular and enjoyable part of English work and not be relegated merely to examination fodder. The organisation of our material in eight sections reflects this principle. Our book is in two parts: *Approaching Poetry* outlines a number of ways in which you can help yourself come to terms with reading, writing and talking about poems. 'I never know what to say' is often the feeling we have when we are suddenly asked to comment upon a poem we have just read; 'Where do I start?' is a common reaction when we are asked to write an essay. The first two sections of the book set out in broad outline how poems express themselves and how you might best approach them. 'How to Read a Poem' shows how a poem is different from any other form of language. Its meanings cannot be summarised; they are a mixture of sounds, rhythms and associations, as well as feelings and ideas, to which you have to be alert and which is yours alone. 'Group Work on a Poem' is a guided way-in to poetry to enable you to read, talk and write positively in a useful sequence of activities. The third section, 'Making Your Own Notes Around a Poem', shows you how to record your thoughts and feelings about a poem you have read. Finally, 'Talking About a Poem' suggests that, after you have made notes about your initial impressions, it is helpful to test your responses against those of others in a small group discussion.

The second part of the book, *Writing About Poetry*, is also arranged in four sections. The first and longest prints several different types of poem — descriptive, lyrical, narrative and so on — and shows how you can reorder your notes ready for writing them up into essay form. 'Comparing Two Poems' has a similar aim where you are asked to deal with two poems at the same time. Some of your work may well entail studying a particular poet: the next short section outlines a way of tackling this task. Finally, we concentrate upon 'Writing for an Examiner' and, through looking at particular examples, we indicate the sorts of ideas and approaches that are likely to improve your performance in formal writing under time pressure.

All eight sections give examples of different ways of working with poems. We hope that these will be discussed with the English teacher in class. Sections 3, 5, 6 and 8 include additional poems for students to work on by themselves. These brief selections need to be augmented from the anthologies the class is using and from other sources.

Michael and Peter Benton

APPROACHING POETRY

Arthur Meighen High School

1 | *How to read a poem*

1. Reading with the eye

Look at any poem laid out on any page — the very presentation invites us to read it with an eye on the length of the lines, the gaps between sections or verses, the spaces around the words. We read poems differently from the way we read fiction. We see most poems *whole*. Try to look at a poem as you might a painting, a photograph on a record sleeve, or a sculpture, and be aware that the lay-out and associations of the words and your *own* view of them are what really matter.

2. Reading with the ear

Read aloud any poem that appeals to you. Poems invite us to speak them with an ear to the rhythm of the lines, the pace of delivery, the sounds of the words. We listen to poems differently from the way we listen to stories. Try to hear the music of the verse as you speak the words.

3. Responding to what is unique

Each poem is highly individual: it needs to be read at least twice. When you have read a poem through both with eye and with ear try to find its heart. It might be an idea, a feeling, the focal point of a description . . . Jot down some notes to capture the poem's distinctive character.

4. Thinking about what is general

Although each poem is unique, all poems have some features in common.
They are:
- made of *words*
- shaped into a particular *form*
- concentrated in their *attention*
- concerned to keep *thinking and feeling* together.

When you are talking or writing about any poem you will find there is something to say about each of these four features.

B Let us see how this sequence of activities works out in practice. Colin wrote 'Dissection' some time during the first few weeks of his sixth form course. He was studying 'A' levels in the Arts and, to complement these, he was required to take three periods of 'minority time' Science each week. His first 'practical' turned out to be the dissection of a rat. No doubt he wrote up his scientific account in the approved manner; but he also wrote the piece on the next page. First, read it silently ('with the eye').

Dissection

This rat looks like it is made of marzipan,
Soft and neatly packaged in its envelope;
I shake it free.
Fingering the damp, yellow fur, I know
That this first touch is far the worst.
     There is a book about it that contains
Everything on a rat, with diagrams
Meticulous, but free from blood
Or all the yellow juices
I will have to pour away.
     Now peg it out:
My pins are twisted and the board is hard
But, using force and fracturing its legs,
I manage though
And crucify my rat.
     From the crutch to the throat the fur is ripped
Not neatly, not as shown in the diagrams,
But raggedly;
My hacking has revealed the body wall
As a sack that is fat with innards to be torn
By the inquisitive eye
And the hand that strips aside.
     Inside this taut, elastic sack is a surprise;
Not the chaos I had thought to find,
No oozing mash; instead of that
A firmly coiled discipline
Of overlapping liver, folded gut;
A neatness that is like a small machine –
And I wonder what it is that has left this rat,
Why a month of probing could not make it go again,
What it is that has disappeared . . .
     The bell has gone; it is time to go for lunch.
I fold the rat, replace it in its bag,
Wash from my hands the sweet
Smell of meat and formalin
And go and eat a meat pie afterwards.
     So, for four weeks or so, I am told,
I shall continue to dissect this rat;
Like a child
Pulling apart a clock he cannot mend.

Colin Rowbotham

Next, read it aloud ('with the ear'). If you are working with one or two others, each of you read out the poem in turn. Read more slowly than the pace of your normal speech. Do not rush this activity; treat it as a performance to be rehearsed and, maybe, discussed.

Now, what is unique about the poem? Without conferring with anyone, spend five minutes or so jotting down your first impressions of "Dissection". What details do you notice, for whatever reason? What is the heart (no pun intended) of it? If you are working in a small group, share these impressions with the others.

Finally, what can you say about the four features we mentioned in A (4) on p. 8? Look at your notes again and see if you can add to them. Four questions which may help are:

- What words, phrases or lines stood out as you read the poem?
- How does the poem develop?
- What has caught Colin's attention, both about the rat and about his own reactions?
- What thoughts and feelings does Colin have during the dissection?

Again, these questions are best tackled first by yourself but try to compare notes with your classmates afterwards.

| C | Some of our jottings in response to these questions are as follows:

Words

The words are direct and uncompromising, not only in action sequences ('Now peg it out . . . ') but also in the continual use of active verbs ("hacking", "strips"). This even extends to the more reflective parts of the poem ("probing", "wash", "pulling apart"). The words are alive with meanings from:

Sounds e.g. the flat 'a' and hard 't's and 'c's of "taut, elastic sack" help to prepare us for the rat as a "small machine"; "oozing" sounds thick and glutinous to go with "mash".

Rhythm — informal movement of speech, but occasional lines have particular rhythmic characters, e.g.

"My pins are twisted and the board is hard" — heavy stresses to suggest physical effort;

"A firmly coiled discipline/Of overlapping liver, folded gut;" — two compact, tightly organised lines to suggest the "small machine";

"And I wonder . . . disappeared . . . " — three longer lines, loosely connected, to suggest the writer's wondering.

Associations — some words hint at other contexts ("elastic sack", "oozing mash"); others jump from the page with their associations ("marzipan" and "crucify").

Form

A monologue; a thoughtful, single voice is speaking. The tone is sympathetic and inviting. The form is not controlled by conventional rhymes and metres yet there's a strong sense of Colin shaping the experience into a narrative. Each detail falls into place as the dissection proceeds; the poem, like the rat, has "a firmly coiled discipline". Both creations have "a neatness that is like a small machine".

Attention

I'm a double eavesdropper — looking over Colin's shoulder as he works at the laboratory bench and listening to his thoughts and feelings.

I'm drawn in to the poem: first I'm made to *look* at objects on the bench — the rat, the package, the fur, the textbook diagrams; then I'm compelled to *see* as I watch the rat pinned out on the board; finally, I'm invited to *perceive* and to share Colin's wonder at "What it is that has disappeared".

Thinking/feeling

When it ends "Like a child/Pulling apart a clock he cannot mend" this sums up Colin's thoughts about the precision and orderliness of the "small machine", his feelings of surprise and pleasure at the discovery, and his unease about his clumsy, destructive actions.

These are *our* jottings. Some of your notes will be similar, some different. However we respond, this poem holds an ironic warning. In probing so closely into the workings of poems, we too run the risk of pulling apart clocks we cannot mend, of losing our pleasure at first reading. It is a difficult balance to hold. In the end, we believe there is a deeper pleasure in *what* is read when this is accompanied by a deeper understanding of *how* this experience has come about.

2 Group work on a poem

You can use the suggestions below as a 'way in' to a poem working either on your own or as a member of a group. We think you will find a group approach most helpful — certainly so at first.

If you are working in a group you may find it makes for a more lively discussion if two or three of you move from A to B to C (all the suggestions in B are mainly to do with how the *language* of the poem works) and for two or three to move from A to C to B (the suggestions in C are mainly to do with *feelings*). Language and feelings cannot really be separated in this way, as you will find once you begin to talk.

Remember, these are only suggestions: you can add to them or shorten them. Some of the ideas will not be much use with some poems. Laid out on the page like this it looks rather a lot to take in and seems all too neat and tidy. Do not worry about it. After using the ideas as a starting-point a few times you will find that you do not need to refer to them very often.

A In groups, if possible, listen to the poem read aloud. On your own and without discussion, jot down any ideas that come to mind immediately after the first reading. Spend no more than 4—5 minutes on this. Don't concern yourselves with "meaning"; concentrate on anything that the poem may remind you of, any feelings, however unexpected, it suggests; any kind of atmosphere. There may be nothing: it doesn't matter.

B Read the poem over to yourselves again — aloud if possible so that you hear it. One member of the group could read the poem or you could share the lines or verses between you. As a group, if possible, underline or circle ideas that occur to you when you ask the following questions. Some people find it very helpful to make notes on the text and jottings in the margin: if you can't do this, a sheet of paper alongside the poem will serve. Share your ideas as a group and talk your way through them after a while:
(i)   Which lines or images did you like or find particularly striking or strange even if you didn't quite understand them?
(ii)   Jot down one or two questions about the poem that you would like answered.
(iii) Look at the poem on the page — at arm's length if you like — what do you notice about its appearance? What is its shape? regular verses? a short single block? sprawling across the page? short lines? long lines? Anything else? The writer decided to present the poem in this way: are there any obvious reasons for his decision?
(iv)   Look more closely. Is it written in a form you recognise such as a *haiku, free verse, rhymed verse, syllabic verse,* a *ballad,* a *sonnet. . .* ? It's quite possible that

you will not recognise a form and it is really not all that important that you should.

(v)   Ring round or note anything that seems to form a pattern. It might be a line, a word or an idea that is repeated from time to time. It might be a sound that is repeated or a mental picture that recurs. There may be comparisons (similes or metaphors) that are repeated. Are any such ideas or images linked or developed in any way?

(vi) What do you notice about the language of the poem? Is there a frequent use of adjectives and/or adverbs — if so, do they have any common theme? Is the poem written in the past, present or future tense? Does the tense change at any point?

(vii) How does the poem seem to 'move'? Do the sound and rhythm of the lines seem light and bubbly, for example, or do the lines move slowly with heavy rounded sounds and a slow rhythm? Are the sounds and rhythms different at different places in the poem? Does the punctuation, or lack of it, help you to see how the poem might be read? Do the lines run on into each other without a break, for example, or are their ends sharply marked by punctuation? Try parts of it out by saying them aloud and listening.

C Read the poem through again and try to think of words that suggest the *mood* of the piece. Does it feel happy, sad, sentimental, defiant, thoughtful, triumphant, unemotional? On your own, jot down the words you think of. Compare yours with those jotted by others in the group. Talk about why you made the choices you did.

(i)   Does the poem seem to develop a line of argument? (For example one line might start with the word "If" and further down there might be a line beginning "Then", "So" or "But" — all words that might advance an argument.) Does it move to a conclusion, a particular point of view at the end? Note any key words in the development of such a line of thought.

(ii) Is it the poet's voice speaking in the poem or is it the voice of somebody else, real or imagined?

(iii) Is the poet speaking out to you? quietly reflecting to himself/herself? addressing the world in general . . . ? If there is another voice in the poem, is it doing the same?

(iv) How does the poet feel about you, the reader? Are you being asked to share something personal? Are you being pleaded with, mocked or laughed at, preached at? Is the poet trying to teach you, persuade you, move you, entertain you . . . something else? How do you know this?

(v)   How does the poet feel about the subject of the poem? Are you being offered a message or a view of things that the writer wants you to share or understand? If so, think about why this might be. Does the poem's title suggest anything about the writer's feelings?

D (i)   Look back at your first notes where you jotted down questions you wanted answering. Have you found answers now? If not, can anyone in the group help?

(ii) Read the poem again in the light of your thoughts and notes. Make any further jottings. Relax. Read it again.

3 | *Making your own notes around a poem*

We have stressed already that reading a poem means 'seeing it whole'. When reading and re-reading, some parts of a poem may seem clear, others hazy; often we seem to find several different points of entry as we build up the details of the picture. We take a sort of mental walk round the poem. We want to encourage you now to use a note-pad on this walk.

Below is an example of the sort of notes that can be made after first reading a poem.

Read Edward Thomas's 'Cock-Crow' first. Then follow our thought-track around the poem.

1st thoughts

– being woken up by two cocks crowing together
– last line
 ⎨ let down feeling
 ⎩ just getting light

2nd thoughts on re-reading

– why 'wood of thoughts'?
– I like the <u>sounds</u> – words and rhymes.
– image chain: wood grows/cut down /axe/cleave/silver blow
– visual impact of heraldic tableau.

6th thoughts

– carefully worked regular shape:
 2 long lines, alt. with broken line. Useful esp. in 'Heralds ... hand, Each... each' = framed.

3rd thoughts

– relation of world in his head and world outside = between visual images and sound of cock-crow.

Cock-Crow

Out of the wood of thoughts that grows by night
To be cut down by the sharp axe of light,
Out of the night, two cocks together crow,
Cleaving the darkness with a silver blow:
And bright before my eyes twin trumpeters stand,
Heralds of splendour, one at either hand,
Each facing each as in a coat of arms:
The milkers lace their boots up at the farms.

Edward Thomas

5th thoughts

lots of opposites like this:

the world	the real world
<u>inside</u> his head . . .	<u>outside</u>
thoughts	. . . actions
night	. . . light
growth	. . . cutting down
darkness	. . . silver

4th thoughts re last 4 lines

contrast between

static	. . . moving
near, local	. . . distanced
stylised	. . . earthy, everyday
colourful	. . . colourless
noble	. . . peasant

Now, make your own notes about one or more of these poems. Try to follow the sequence of first thoughts, second thoughts etc., as we have done.

Poplar

propped up
against the pale
wall of the sky,
small birds
snipped from
black paper
pose there
in silhouette:
summer's dark plume is
winter's besom broom

Gerda Mayer

Shantytown

High on the veld upon that plain
And far from streets and lights and cars
And bare of trees, and bare of grass,
Jabavu sleeps beneath the stars.

Jabavu sleeps.
The children cough.
Cold creeps up, the hard night cold,
The earth is tight within its grasp,
The highveld cold without soft rain,
Dry as the sand, rough as a rasp
The frost rimmed night invades the shacks.
Through dusty ground
Through rocky ground
Through freezing ground the night cold creeps.
In cotton blankets, rags and sacks
Beneath the stars Jabavu sleeps.

One day Jabavu will awake
To greet a new and shining day;
The sound of coughing will become
The children's laughter as they play
In parks with flowers where dust now swirls
In strong-walled homes with warmth and light.
But for tonight Jabavu sleeps.
Jabavu sleeps. The stars are bright.

Anonymous (South Africa)

The Warm and the Cold

Freezing dusk is closing
  Like a slow trap of steel
On trees and roads and hills and all
  That can no longer feel.
      But the carp is in its depth
        Like a planet in its heaven,
      And the badger in its bedding
        Like a loaf in the oven.
      And the butterfly in its mummy
        Like a viol in its case.
      And the owl in its feathers
        Like a doll in its lace.

Freezing dusk has tightened
  Like a nut screwed tight
On the starry aeroplane
  Of the soaring night.
      But the trout is in its hole
        Like a chuckle in a sleeper.
      The hare strays down the highway
        Like a root going deeper.
      The snail is dry in the outhouse
        Like a seed in a sunflower.
      The owl is pale on the gatepost
        Like a clock on its tower.

Moonlight freezes the shaggy world
  Like a mammoth of ice –
The past and the future
  Are the jaws of a steel vice.
      But the cod is in the tide-rip
        Like a key in a purse.
      The deer are on the bare-blown hill
        Like smiles on a nurse.
      The flies are behind the plaster
        Like the lost score of a jig.
      Sparrows are in the ivy-clump
        Like money in a pig.

Such a frost
  The flimsy moon
    Has lost her wits.

      A star falls.

The sweating farmers
  Turn in their sleep
    Like oxen on spits.

Ted Hughes

4 | Talking about a poem

A group of five students talked about "The Warm and the Cold" (p. 16). We thought it would be helpful to you in your own groups to eavesdrop on parts of their conversation and to test out your ideas of the poem against theirs.

They had some questions which you may be able to answer; they may have some answers to questions you have raised.

Reading written–down speech is difficult if you are not used to it. Why not cast it and read it as a play?

Extract 1

Graham	'a chuckle in a sleeper.' What's a 'chuckle in a sleeper'?*
Tom	Oh yes.
Nick	Well, a sleeper could be —
Zoe	A railway sleeper —
Graham	A railway sleeper, yeah, so a chuckle might be —
Tom	Yeah — or a sleeper can be a person sleeping.
Graham	Or a train. *(laughter)*
Tom	I mean — erm —
Zoe	What's the chuckle bit then?

* What do you think it means?

Extract 2

Zoe	'The past and the future/Are the jaws of a steel vice.'
Nick	That's pretty stupid.
Tom	Yeah. Suppose it could mean the two things coming together.
Zoe	It's being held together.
Tom	Yeah, well the two things, the past and the future, coming together into the present —
Nick	Means you can't separate them*. — You can't really, can you?
Zoe	Well they're frozen together.

* Nick begins to see an idea in the line Zoe quotes.
Can you take it further?

Extract 3

Graham	'Such a frost/The flimsy moon/Has lost her wits' —
Zoe	— and then 'the sweating farmers' —
Graham	Yeah, and then he breaks it with 'A star falls'
Zoe	Yes
Graham	'A star falls' —
Tom	I wonder why he did that — break it with 'A star falls'?*
Zoe	Why is there 'A star falls'?

* Why do you think the structure of the poem changes here?

Extract 4

Graham	'The deer on the. . .'. What about 'The deer are on the bare-blown hill/Like smiles on a nurse'?
Zoe	I don't get that.
Graham	No, it doesn't seem like all this. The others kind of relate — the cod, and the key in the purse, kind of relate more than 'the deer on . . .'
Tom	Yeah, What is . . . I mean it's got fish in all three here — 'the carp's in its depth/Like a planet in its heaven' then 'the trout's in its hole/Like a chuckle in a sleeper' — erm — and 'the cod's in the tide — rip/Like a key in a purse.' It must all relate somehow.
Graham	The first verse is always fish — . . . Up here you've got the first four lines then you've got fish.*

* Can you see any other patterns?

Extract 5

Nick	One thing about this poem is that it's a lot of effort to read it —
Graham	Yeah
Tom	Yeah. Some poems —
Zoe	— On your own. It's not so much effort when you're doing it all together but on your own — to get right into it like we have done —
Graham	But in class —
Tom	— we wouldn't bother really looking.
Graham	— you can't really say what you want to say if you've got a teacher in there, because the teacher's got their own ideas on it, hasn't he?
Tom	Exactly! Exactly! They don't really listen to us a lot.
Lucy	You can't analyse it just by first look — you have to go into it.
Tom	You've got to read it.
Zoe	You've got to go into it*.
Tom	Yeah. They can put forward their ideas — say what they — say what they think about it, you know — but they should, they should let us have a go as well. It's no good just saying — er — 'Do you agree with me?' You're bound to say yes.
Zoe	And you daren't say no.
Tom	And normally you're asked to write a poem . . .

* Do *you* have any ideas about the best way of tackling poems?

WRITING ABOUT POETRY

5 | *Studying single poems*

In the first part of the book we have concentrated upon reading, talking and note-making as basic activities in approaching poetry. Now we want to help you organise your ideas towards more formal writing by building upon these 'basics'.

With each of three examples in turn carry out the following sequence of activities *before* you move on to our notes.

Reading. Read the poem silently; read it aloud as a member of a small group. Charles Causley's poem can be shared between two voices; "Metaphors" might be read one line per person around a group.

Note-making. Individually, make your own notes around the poems, as in section 3 (p. 14).

Drafting. Use your notes to answer these three questions about each poem:

A What sort of poem is it? B How does it work? C What do I feel about it?

Spring Pools

These pools that, though in forests, still reflect
The total sky almost without defect,
And like the flowers beside them, chill and shiver,
Will like the flowers beside them soon be gone,
And yet not out by any brook or river,
But up by roots to bring dark foliage on.

The trees that have it in their pent-up buds
To darken nature and be summer woods –
Let them think twice before they use their powers
To blot out and drink up and sweep away
These flowery waters and these watery flowers
From snow that melted only yesterday.

Robert Frost

Metaphors

I'm a riddle in nine syllables,
An elephant, a ponderous house,
A melon strolling on two tendrils.
O red fruit, ivory, fine timbers!
This loaf's big with its yeasty rising.
Money's new-minted in this fat purse.
I'm a means, a stage, a cow in calf.
I've eaten a bag of green apples,
Boarded the train there's no getting off.

Sylvia Plath

Mary, Mary Magdalene

*On the east wall of the church of St Mary Magdalene at Launceston
in Cornwall is a granite figure of the saint. The children of the town
say that a stone lodged on her back will bring good luck.*

Mary, Mary Magdalene
Lying on the wall,
I throw a pebble on your back.
Will it lie or fall?

Send me down for Christmas
Some stockings and some hose,
And send before the winter's end
A brand-new suit of clothes.

Mary, Mary Magdalene
Under a stony tree,
I throw a pebble on your back.
What will you send me?

   I'll send you for your christening
   A woollen robe to wear,
   A shiny cup from which to sup,
   And a name to bear.

Mary, Mary Magdalene
Lying cool as snow,
What will you be sending me
When to school I go?

   I'll send a pencil and a pen
   That write both clean and neat,
   And I'll send to the schoolmaster
   A tongue that's kind and sweet.

Mary, Mary Magdalene
Lying in the sun,
What will you be sending me
Now I'm twenty-one?

   I'll send you down a locket
   As silver as your skin,
   And I'll send you a lover
   To fit a gold key in.

Mary, Mary Magdalene
Underneath the spray,
What will you be sending me
On my wedding-day?

   I'll send you down some blossom,
   Some ribbons and some lace,
   And for the bride a veil to hide
   The blushes on her face.

Mary, Mary Magdalene
Whiter than the swan,
Tell me what you'll send me,
Now my good man's dead and gone.

   I'll send to you a single bed
   On which you must lie,
   And pillows bright where tears may light
   That fall from your eye.

Mary, Mary Magdalene
Now nine months are done,
What will you be sending me
For my little son?

   I'll send you for your baby
   A lucky stone, and small,
   To throw to Mary Magdalene
   Lying on the wall.

                 Charles Causley

Now, compare your notes with ours on the following pages.

Spring Pools

Annotations (left):
Immediately invites us to look, to create the image of these pools here and now in our mind's eye. Writer addresses us as though we were at his side seeing what he sees.

These pools that, though in forests, still reflect

The total sky almost without defect,

And like the flowers beside them, chill and shiver,

Will like the flowers beside them soon be gone,

And yet not out by any brook or river,

But up by roots to bring dark foliage on.

Poem splits here: 1st 6 lines on pools, 2nd 6 lines on trees.
Rhyme scheme identical (a,a,b,c,b,c); same rhythm

The trees that have it in their pent-up buds

To darken nature and be summer woods -

Let them think twice before they use their powers

To blot out and drink up and sweep away

These flowery waters and these watery flowers

From snow that melted only yesterday.

Robert Frost

Right annotations:
Early spring; no leaves. Eyes move from focus down on pools to up to down.

clipped 'i' sounds suggest coldness and delicacy

? almost magical

Eye moves up

Balanced mirror image.

- suggest possibility.
- potential.
- pent-up suggests only just held in check, imprisoned.
- heavy. Unusually, summer not seen as 'good' opposed to winter as 'evil'. Summer darkens nature. Even-handed cyclical. magical.

But note their turn will come.

delicate, transient image.

Left annotations (lower):
almost human ? magical

blot out sky
blot up pools
(as blotting paper)
blot out reflected image.

cf. line 3

hint of menace, the snow melted only recently. It will inevitably return and subdue the summer woods. Natural rhythm and pattern of the year. The balance of the poem's structure suggest this balanced pattern in nature.

A What sort of poem is it?
B How does it work?
C What do I feel about it?

A • It's descriptive. A straightforward description of pools of water beneath trees in early spring.
   • It's reflective (in more ways than one!) and suggests the never-ending cyclical pattern of the seasons.
B • Conversational tone buttonholes us and makes us see with the poet's eye.
   • Structure of poem important. It is delicately and precisely balanced like the balance of the seasons: it's a mirror image in each half between pools and sky, flowers and tree tops.
   • It is suggestive of dark, almost magical natural forces. Beneath the delicate surface there is a hint of menace.
C • I like its surface simplicity, even more the suggestion that it is about more than its surface suggests — that it represents something deeper to do with human life not just the pattern of the seasons. There's a sense of threat towards the end but, on reflection, it's more a bowing to the inevitable and is perhaps more comforting than menacing — a recognition of the patterns to which we are all subject.

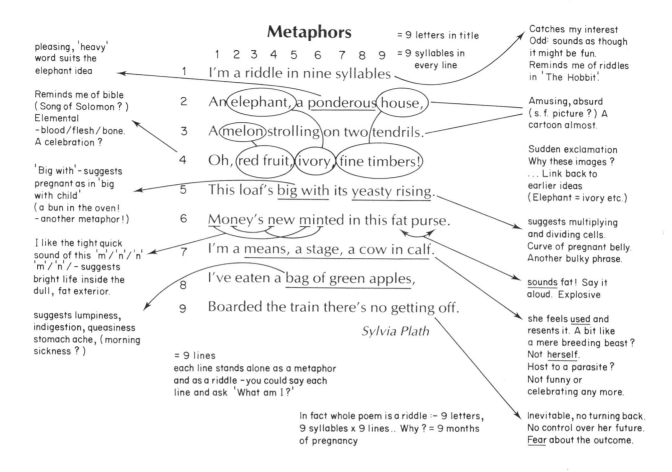

Metaphors

= 9 letters in title

Catches my interest
Odd: sounds as though
it might be fun.
Reminds me of riddles
in 'The Hobbit'.

pleasing, 'heavy'
word suits the
elephant idea

1 2 3 4 5 6 7 8 9   = 9 syllables in every line

1 I'm a riddle in nine syllables.

Reminds me of bible
(Song of Solomon ?)
Elemental
– blood / flesh / bone.
A celebration ?

2 An elephant, a ponderous house,

Amusing, absurd
(s. f. picture ?) A
cartoon almost.

3 A melon strolling on two tendrils.

4 Oh, red fruit, ivory, fine timbers!

Sudden exclamation
Why these images ?
… Link back to
earlier ideas
(Elephant = ivory etc.)

'Big with' – suggests
pregnant as in 'big
with child'
(a bun in the oven!
– another metaphor!)

5 This loaf's big with its yeasty rising.

suggests multiplying
and dividing cells.
Curve of pregnant belly.
Another bulky phrase.

6 Money's new minted in this fat purse.

I like the tight quick
sound of this 'm'/'n'/'n'
'm'/'n'/ – suggests
bright life inside the
dull, fat exterior.

7 I'm a means, a stage, a cow in calf.

sounds fat! Say it
aloud. Explosive

8 I've eaten a bag of green apples,

she feels used and
resents it. A bit like
a mere breeding beast ?
Not herself.
Host to a parasite ?
Not funny or
celebrating any more.

suggests lumpiness,
indigestion, queasiness
stomach ache, (morning
sickness ?)

9 Boarded the train there's no getting off.

Sylvia Plath

= 9 lines
each line stands alone as a metaphor
and as a riddle – you could say each
line and ask 'What am I ?'

In fact whole poem is a riddle :– 9 letters,
9 syllables x 9 lines.. Why ? = 9 months
of pregnancy

Inevitable, no turning back.
No control over her future.
Fear about the outcome.

A What sort of poem is it?
B How does it work?
C What do I feel about it?

A *Mixed feelings about pregnancy.*
- Begins in detached, half-joking way; something of a game; sees herself as a faintly absurd cartoon figure (lines 1−3).
- Moves to what is almost a joyful, celebratory view of pregnancy (l. 4).
- Away from this high point, in lines 4 and 6, doubts begin to creep in with one image in each line positive, the other less so. Physical revulsion sets in.
- Leaves us with an increasing sense of desperation. She feels used, resentful and fearful.

Overall, the powerful negative images with which the poem leaves us prevail, though the other more positive aspects of her pregnancy are still glimpsed through the turmoil.

B
- Primarily through metaphors as the title suggests. Each line is a self-contained metaphor. The structure of the poem with its nine lines and nine syllables per line is itself a metaphor for the nine months of pregnancy.
- Strong visual images such as 'a melon strolling on two tendrils'.
- Complex patterns of associations and tight network of images as for example

lines 2, 3, 4. Images of heaviness, bulkiness predominate and appear in seven out of nine lines. Strongly physical.

- Strong emphasis on sounds echoing sense. For example lines 2, 5, 6.
- It's dramatic, speaks personally and directly to the reader. ("I'm a riddle . . . ") and engages interest by its riddling.
- We share her confusion — it's deliberately disorientating at first reading — and re-enact her emotions as they develop over the nine lines.

C • After initial uncertainty, a sense of pleasure at having cracked the puzzle. On re-reading a growing sense of dismay and a sharing of her fears coupled with great admiration for the technical skill, the control which allows her to move me through such a range of emotions in so short a space. I don't know the tumultuous mental state of being pregnant: I feel I understand this more now. The poem enlarges my experience.

Mary, Mary Magdalene

On the east wall of the church of St Mary Magdalene at Launceston in Cornwall is a granite figure of the saint. The children of the town say that a stone lodged on her back will bring good luck.

Mary, Mary Magdalene
Lying on the wall,
I throw a pebble on your back.
Will it lie or fall?

Send me down for Christmas
Some stockings and some hose,
And send before the winter's end
A brand-new suit of clothes.

Mary, Mary Magdalene
Under a stony tree,
I throw a pebble on your back.
What will you send me?

*I'll send you for your christening
A woollen robe to wear,
A shiny cup from which to sup,
And a name to bear.*

Mary, Mary Magdalene
Lying cool as snow,
What will you be sending me
When to school I go?

*I'll send a pencil and a pen
That write both clean and neat,
And I'll send to the schoolmaster
A tongue that's kind and sweet.*

Who is speaking? A child's voice, chanting a rhyme. What is happening? Child throws a pebble on to the stone figure of the saint. / Local superstition and Christian belief brought together. Sing-song rhythm / nursery rhymes / games.

Child makes wishes (pebble must have stayed there). Oddly old-fashioned feel about Christmas wishes for clothes. 'Hose', too, is archaic; and 'stockings' and 'brand new suit' for a young child. Edwardian feel.

1st age: the baby

More stone decoration 'stony tree'. The first question addressed to M.M.

Who is speaking? M.M. replies: the good luck for the baby is to be named, to be clothed and to be fed - the basics of life.

2nd age: the schoolgirl

Child-like urgency in repeated 1st line address to saint and insistent questions. M.M. 'cool as snow' suggests innocence of childhood; perhaps the white granite, too. The coolness is emphasised by internal rhyme of 'cool'-'school' as well as the normal end rhymes.

Maternal care in saint's language: 'clean', 'neat', 'kind', 'sweet'.

Mary, Mary Magdalene
Lying in the sun,
What will you be sending me
Now I'm twenty-one?

I'll send you down a locket
As silver as your skin,
And I'll send you a lover
To fit a gold key in.

Mary, Mary Magdalene
Underneath the spray,
What will you be sending me
On my wedding-day?

I'll send you down some blossom,
Some ribbons and some lace,
And for the bride a veil to hide
The blushes on her face.

Mary, Mary Magdalene
Whiter than the swan,
Tell me what you'll send me,
Now my good man's dead and gone.

I'll send to you a single bed
On which you must lie,
And pillows bright where tears may light
That fall from your eye.

Mary, Mary Magdalene
Now nine months are done,
What will you be sending me
For my little son?

I'll send you for your baby
A lucky stone, and small,
To throw to Mary Magdalene
Lying on the wall.

Charles Causley

3rd age: the lover

Saint's figure is now seen as warm in the sun; suits the woman anticipating her lover.

Sexual imagery: gold key/silver locket; sensuality of 'skin'.

4th age: the bride

Another bit of stonework: 'spray' part of 'the stony tree'?

Feeling of rich, summery colours: 'blossom', 'ribbons', 'blushes' to celebrate the wedding—balanced by the coyness/reserve of the internal rhyme 'bride'... 'hide'.

5th age: the widow

The white/swan link suggests death (contrast snow in vs.5). Solemn note-'...good man's dead and gone'-down-to-earth, matter-of-fact acceptance; old-fashioned, rustic 'feel'.

Loneliness of 'single bed'; sadness of loss of loved one. Curious 'bright'/'light' internal rhyme makes the weeping into the pillow stylised rather than 'felt emotion'. Ritual grieving/mourning suggest inevitability of death; no sentimentality.

6th age: the mother

The cycle starts again. Normally, we'd expect 5th/6th ages in reverse order. This way Causley can complete the cycle with new born baby.

M.M. ends poem both optimistically ('lucky stone'), and yet resigned to inevitability of cycle of life and death.

A What sort of poem is it?
B How does it work?
C What do I feel about it?

A • It is a story shared between two voices, those of the girl and the saint; a story that ends where it began.
  • It plots the 'six ages of woman'. The poem is organised in pairs of verses which, after the introductory pair, alternate the voices of the girl and the Saint in the six subsequent pairs.

- Its language and form are those of a ballad. Descriptions are clear and unqualified by adjectives and adverbs; objects are included simply to stand for one of the 'ages', not for detailed description. The form is like that of a nursery rhyme.

B   My detailed notes above would lead me to expand on these three points — perhaps a paragraph on each:

- *the story of the poem.* The life-cycle marked by its main turning-points/ceremonies. It's circular: by reversing 'widow' and 'mother', Causley can complete one cycle with a new born baby and simultaneously imply the start of another.

- *the shape of the poem.* The first two verses set up the situation of making wishes when the pebble lodges on the stone saint. Then each subsequent pair focusses in turn on the baby, the schoolgirl, the lover, the bride, the widow and the mother. It's as regular and ordered as a ritual.

- *the language of the poem.* An old-fashioned (Edwardian?) feel (vs. 2) seems to distance the poem in time. The girl's description of the saint (first verse of each pair) changes according to the 'age' ("under a stony tree" for the baby vs. 3; "cool as snow" for the schoolgirl vs. 5; "lying in the sun" for the lover vs. 7, etc. . . .). Mary Magdalene's reply is characterised by appropriate objects (name, clothes, food for baby vs. 4; pencil and pen for schoolgirl vs. 6; sexual imagery of key and locket for lover vs. 8, etc. . . .) which are emblems for that 'age'.

C   Overall, it's a poem I like for its order and completeness. It's not personal; the poet doesn't tell me directly about his feelings. But I do get a sense of his ambivalent feelings at the end about the cycle of life he has described. For the poem ends optimistically with the "lucky stone" and the idea of growth and continuity; yet there's the sense of resigned inevitability at the cycle of life and death in the last verse. Increasingly, too, the bright, lively tone of the nursery rhyme rhythms are offset by the growing sense that human life falls into a pattern we have to accept.

The poems on this and the next two pages should be approached through the same sequence of activities.

The Sick Rose

O Rose thou art sick.
The invisible worm,
That flies in the night
In the howling storm:

Has found out thy bed
Of crimson joy:
And his dark secret love
Does thy life destroy.

William Blake

In a Station of the Metro

The apparition of these faces in the crowd;
Petals on a wet, black bough.

Ezra Pound

Mirror

I am silver and exact. I have no preconceptions.
Whatever I see I swallow immediately
Just as it is, unmisted by love or dislike.
I am not cruel, only truthful —
The eye of a little god, four-cornered.
Most of the time I meditate on the opposite wall.
It is pink, with speckles. I have looked at it so long
I think it is a part of my heart. But it flickers.
Faces and darkness separate us over and over.

Now I am a lake. A woman bends over me,
Searching my reaches for what she really is.
Then she turns to those liars, the candles or the moon.
I see her back, and reflect it faithfully.
She rewards me with tears and an agitation of hands.
I am important to her. She comes and goes.
Each morning it is her face that replaces the darkness.
In me she has drowned a young girl, and in me an old woman
Rises toward her day after day, like a terrible fish.

Sylvia Plath

Nothing Gold Can Stay

Nature's first green is gold,
Her hardest hue to hold.
Her early leaf's a flower;
But only so an hour.
Then leaf subsides to leaf.
So Eden sank to grief,
So dawn goes down to day.
Nothing gold can stay.

Robert Frost

Why I Gave You The Chinese Plate

for Kenny Storrie

I know how you feel
about ladies that are dark and slim
and quiet and unlike me.
And chinoiserie.

I'm not sorry.
Neither are you what
I'd have thought I wanted.

In a landscape somewhere else
under a surface finely crazed with cracks
the silks of this painted girl instead
of all the dark girls you'll never have
as long as you keep wanting me to love.

Goldgreen, plum and jade
a nice glaze.
So choose
Where you'll hang it
on the wall we might tear down.

Liz Lochhead

6 | Comparing two poems

A The problem

You may be asked as part of your course work or in preparation for an exam to choose two poems on the same topic from a thematic anthology and compare them, or you may be given two unseen poems and asked to write about their similarities and differences. Both tasks can lead to confusion if you do not have a clear idea of how to tackle them. How do you organise your work? Do you write two separate, short essays and put them together? Do you flit back and forth between the poems?

B Preparation

We suggest a four-phase approach:
(i)   Read both poems once for overall sense of theme, treatment and the nature of the relationship between the two poems.
(ii) Re-read poem A and make quick jottings on the situation and the nature of the poem, its 'voice', words, images, ideas, feelings etc. . . . (as in section 3, p. 14). Re-read poem B and do likewise.
(iii) Say what is unique to each poem with brief supporting evidence. No more than three or four lines here to 'capture' each poem.
(iv) List the main points of similarity and difference between the two poems.

C Writing up

This preparation should enable you to structure an essay as follows:
• Opening paragraph, based upon (iii) above, which captures the quality and nature of the two poems.
• Several subsequent paragraphs, based upon (ii) above, which discuss the details you noticed in your reading of the poems. It is usually best to concentrate first on poem A, then on poem B, just as you did in the note-making.
• Final paragraph, based upon (iv) above, which discusses the main points of similarity and difference and, if appropriate, indicates the reasons for your preference of one poem over the other.

D An example

Compare the following two poems. Carry out the four-phase preparation *before* you look ahead to our notes.

Read the poems (phase 1)

The Tom-cat

At midnight in the alley
  A Tom-cat comes to wail,
And he chants the hate of a million years
  As he swings his snaky tail.

Malevolent, bony, brindled,
  Tiger and devil and bard,
His eyes are coals from the middle of Hell
  And his heart is black and hard.

He twists and crouches and capers
  And bares his curved sharp claws,
And he sings to the stars of the jungle nights,
  Ere cities were, or laws.

Beast from a world primeval,
  He and his leaping clan,
When the blotched red moon leers over the roofs
  Give voice to their scorn of man.

He will lie on a rug to-morrow
  And lick his silky fur,
And veil the brute in his yellow eyes
  And play he's tame and purr.

But at midnight in the alley
  He will crouch again and wail,
And beat the time for his demon's song
  With the swing of his demon's tail.

Don Marquis

Esther's Tomcat

Daylong this tomcat lies stretched flat
As an old rough mat, no mouth and no eyes.
Continual wars and wives are what
Have tattered his ears and battered his head.

Like a bundle of old rope and iron
Sleeps till blue dusk. Then reappear
His eyes, green as ringstones: he yawns wide red,
Fangs fine as a lady's needle and bright.

A tomcat sprang at a mounted knight,
Locked round his neck like a trap of hooks
While the knight rode fighting its clawing and bite.
After hundreds of years the stain's there

On the stone where he fell, dead of the tom:
That was at Barnborough. The tomcat still
Grallochs[1] odd dogs on the quiet,   [1]disembowels
Will take the head clean off your simple pullet,

Is unkillable. From the dog's fury,
From gunshot fired point-blank he brings
His skin whole, and whole
From owlish moons of bekittenings

Among ashcans. He leaps and lightly
Walks upon sleep, his mind on the moon
Nightly over the round world of men,
Over the roofs go his eyes and outcry.

Ted Hughes

Notes around the poems (phase 2)

The whole poem reads like an incantation:
it has the pace and rhythm of a chant.
Line 3 of each verse has extra syllables
and more varied musicality.

The cat emerges from a
double darkness:–
'wailing in local setting
of the alley;

The Tom-cat

At midnight in the alley
   A Tom-cat comes to wail,
And he chants the hate of a million years
   As he swings his snaky tail.

'hating' in historical
setting as a devilish
creature with 'snaky tail'

Strong physical presence
Metaphorical presence

Malevolent, bony, brindled,
   Tiger and devil and bard,
His eyes are coals from the middle of Hell
   And his heart is black and hard.

melodramatic piratical,
diabolic portrait.

He's a 'primitive' in his
movements (l.1), his
song (l.3) and his
origins (ll.3 and 4)

He twists and crouches and capers
   And bares his curved sharp claws,
And he sings to the stars of the jungle nights,
   Ere cities were, or laws.

He's an aggressive
primitive, threatening
the urban with the law
of the jungle.

He's associated with the
moon and stars; cosmic
world is 'in the know'

Cat as 'primeval beast'
that scorns human
civilisation.

Beasts from a world primeval,
   He and his leaping clan,
When the blotched red moon leers over the roofs
   Give voice to their scorn of man.

Contrast the daytime
cat:–
'purrs' for 'wails'.
'Picks + lies' for 'twists
+ crouches', 'silky fur'
for 'bony' + 'sharp claws'

Tame domestic presence
masking the brute
within.

He will lie on a rug to-morrow
   And lick his silky fur,
And veil the brute in his yellow eyes
   And play he's tame and purr.

But at midnight in the alley
   He will crouch again and wail,
And beat the time for his demon's song
   With the swing of his demon's tail.

Don Marquis

We're left with the
diabolic cat again –
all the primitive elements
– setting, time, sounds
and movement.

31

Examining poetry

Esther's Tomcat

Daylong this tomcat lies stretched flat
As an old rough mat, no mouth and no eyes
Continual wars and wives are what
Have tattered his ears and battered his head.

Like a bundle of old rope and iron
Sleeps till blue dusk. Then reappear
His eyes, green as ringstones: he yawns wide red,
Fangs fine as a lady's needle and bright.

A tomcat sprang at a mounted knight
Locked round his neck like a trap of hooks
While the knight rode fighting its clawing and bite.
After hundreds of years the stain's there

On the stone where he fell, dead of the tom:
That was at Barnborough. The tomcat still
Grallochs' odd dogs on the quiet,
Will take the head clean of your simple pullet,

Is unkillable. From the dog's fury,
From gunshot fired point-blank he brings
His skin whole, and whole
From owlish moons of bekittenings

Among ashcans. He leaps and lightly
Walks upon sleep, his mind on the moon
Nightly over the round world of men,
Over the roofs go his eyes and outcry.

Ted Hughes

Annotations:

Who is Esther? Daughter, little girl, woman?
Contrast between female and male principles

'Hard' sounds, flat, short vowels, uncompromising, suggests toughness.

Interesting rhymes and half rhymes hold it together along with repeated hard consonants. Strong stresses in each line; no clear stress pattern but 4 main ones each line. No clear rhyme pattern to its theme.

Suggests strength despite being inert.

reminds me of ballads 'green', 'red', 'bright', 'lady' – provides link to medieval story in next verse.

Suggests tomcat's audacity and strength

A story interpolated. Medieval (= the tom has been around for centuries; it's a survivor) Notice all the 't' sounds.

He leaves his mark

'disembowels' = tears the guts from; vicious sounding word

Uncompromising flat statement

open ended

Invited to see Tomcat before us: 'this' tomcat. Conversational to some extent.

no pronoun, tough emeralds?
Note contrast between these 'fine' images and dull, moth-eaten ones earlier.

Conversational tone
Almost casual killing
Conversational

Physical strength; a suggestion of magical power?

Suggests his sexual strength.

Neat let down from grand line to 'ashcan'

Almost suggests he's outside our little world.

32

What is each poem's character? (phase 3)

(i) "The Tom-cat" is seen as a demonic creature, *viz*:
   - diabolic tail he swings in vss. 1 and 6
   - primitive incantation of rhyme and metre of the verses
   - associations with darkness of midnight and pre-history
   - strong physical presence.

   All of this threatens the comfortable, domestic city world.

(ii) "Esther's Tomcat" has a sense of strength, independence and overwhelming maleness. He's outside the normal laws of nature; a survivor from an older world, drawing his power from a savage past. Yet, for all that, he's still deceptively domestic — he's Esther's tomcat.

Some points of similarity and difference (phase 4)

- Both have the idea that beneath surface appearance exists a violent, cruel nature — something that takes its power from a savage history. Both contrast the domestic cat with the feral beast.
- Although both poems consist of six four-line verses they are formally quite different. Don Marquis's poem is highly organised in terms of metre and rhyme; the verses are self-contained. Ted Hughes's has no regular metrical pattern but is based on four stresses per line which helps the flat, matter-of-fact tone of the poem. There is no regular rhyme pattern but lots of repeated hard consonants, especially the 't' sounds. Also, the verses are often run–on, not self-contained. The form of Marquis's poem dominates the cat; Esther's tomcat will not be controlled.
- Marquis's poem has a chanting tone, song-like, polished, neatly-packaged. The skill of the performance neuters the image of the tom–cat as a threatening devil: he's more of a pantomime figure. Hughes's poem gains a lot from being a series of flat statements; the violence is stronger through the plain, blunt speaking.
- Vs. 1 of Hughes's poem and vs. 5 of Marquis's poem give corresponding pictures yet they're very different. This is where the contrast between the poems shows.

E Try out the approach of the previous pages with the following pairs of poems.

(i) **A Negro Woman**

carrying a bunch of marigolds
    wrapped
        in an old newspaper:
She carries them upright,
    bareheaded,
        the bulk
of her thighs
    causing her to waddle
        as she walks
looking into
    the store window which she passes
        on her way.
What is she
    but an ambassador
        from another world
a world of pretty marigolds
    of two shades
        which she announces
not knowing what she does
    other
        than walk the streets
holding the flowers upright
    as a torch
        so early in the morning.

William Carlos Williams

34

The Fat Black Woman Goes Shopping

Shopping in London winter
is a real drag for the fat black woman
going from store to store
in search of accommodating clothes
and de weather so cold

Look at the frozen thin mannequins
fixing her with grin
and de pretty face salesgals
exchanging slimming glances
thinking she don't notice

Lord is aggravating

Nothing soft and bright and billowing
to flow like breezy sunlight
when she walking

The fat black woman curses in Swahili/Yoruba
and nation language under her breathing
all this journeying and journeying

The fat black woman could only conclude
that when it come to fashion
the choice is lean

Nothing much beyond size 14

Grace Nichols

(ii)   ## The Send-off

Down the close, darkening lanes they sang their way
To the siding-shed,
And lined the train with faces grimly gay.

Their breasts were stuck all white with wreath and spray
As men's are, dead.

Dull porters watched them, and a casual tramp
Stood staring hard,
Sorry to miss them from the upland camp.
Then, unmoved, signals nodded, and a lamp
Winked to the guard.

So secretly, like wrongs hushed-up, they went.
They were not ours:
We never heard to which front these were sent.

Nor there if they yet mock what women meant
Who gave them flowers.

Shall they return to beatings of great bells
In wild train-loads?
A few, a few, too few for drums and yells,
May creep back, silent, to village wells
Up half-known roads.

Wilfred Owen

Men Who March Away

Song of the Soldiers

What of the faith and fire within us
      Men who march away
      Ere the barn-cocks say
      Night is growing grey,
Leaving all that here can win us;
What of the faith and fire within us
      Men who march away?

Is it a purblind prank, O think you,
      Friend with the musing eye,
      Who watch us stepping by
      With doubt and dolorous sigh?
Can much pondering so hoodwink you!
Is it a purblind prank, O think you,
      Friend with the musing eye?

Nay. We well see what we are doing,
      Though some may not see—
      Dalliers as they be—
      England's need are we;
Her distress would leave us rueing:
Nay. We well see what we are doing,
      Though some may not see!

In our heart of hearts believing
      Victory crowns the just,
      And that braggarts must
      Surely bite the dust,
Press we to the field ungrieving,
In our heart of hearts believing
      Victory crowns the just.

Hence the faith and fire within us
      Men who march away
      Ere the barn-cocks say
      Night is growing grey,
Leaving all that here can win us;
Hence the faith and fire within us
      Men who march away.

Thomas Hardy

7 | *Studying a poet's work*

Commonly, fifteen or twenty poems by a single author are required reading when studying for an exam. Among the most popular poets for study are R. S. Thomas, Ted Hughes, Charles Causley, John Betjeman, Robert Frost and Seamus Heaney. The following sequence of activities aims to help you come to terms with a body of poems by one poet.

A Reading — in groups.

- Groups choose up to three poems on which to concentrate.
- Read each poem silently and aloud. Look for opportunities to use more than one voice per poem.
- An LP recording or cassette tape may be available. Try to hear it.
- Talk about your first impressions of the poems. List any questions that you would like answered.
- Prepare a reading of one of the poems for the rest of the class. (See D below.)

B Note-making — on your own.

- Individually, make your own notes around each of the 3 poems (as in section 3 p. 14).

C Sharing impressions — in groups.

- Groups pool individual ideas.
    What is each poem about?
    How is it said?
    What feelings does it leave you with?
- List any common themes, attitudes or ways of writing that recur. It may help to underline phrases that seem characteristic of this poet.

D Putting ideas together — whole class.

- Each group presents the prepared reading (from A above) to the rest of the class.
- Each group talks about what they have found of interest in this poem and, where appropriate, the other two poems.
- Individuals jot down their own notes and ask questions.

- The class should now be able to summarise the main characteristics of the poet's writing.
- This may be a good point at which to seek further information about the poet from other sources. Questions that it may be helpful to ask may be about the circumstances in which the poems were written, the period, background, setting or the poet's personal life.

E Focussing your ideas – for groups or individuals

The following activities will help you to a better understanding of a particular writer's work:
- compiling a folder on the reading you have done, the life and background of the poet, what appeal you find in his/her work and, perhaps, some of your own poems;
- creating a wall display to capture what you think is the spirit of the poet's work;
- making a short taped anthology of the best reading you can manage of a selection of poems.
  You may want to introduce and link the poems with your own comments and background information.

8 | Writing for an examiner

Questions on poems vary from one examination board to another. You may be asked in very general terms to write an essay about an unseen poem, or you may be required to answer a list of comprehension questions about specific details.

We make no attempt to cover all the possibilities. Rather we concentrate upon an example from the Cambridge Plain Texts Paper,

(i) because this approach reflects our emphasis upon personal response throughout this book; and

(ii) because if you adopt this approach it provides a good grounding from which you can tackle examination questions which direct you to more particular aspects of a poem.

Here is a poem printed with the instructions from the examiner exactly as it appeared on the examination paper:

Read through the following poem at least once, to get the sense of it.

Born Yesterday

Tightly folded bud,
I have wished you something
None of the others would:
Not the usual stuff
About being beautiful,
Or running off a spring
Of innocence or love —
They will all wish you that,
And should it prove possible,
Well, you're a lucky girl.

But if it shouldn't, then
May you be ordinary;
Have like other women
An average of talents:
Not ugly, not good-looking,
Nothing uncustomary
To pull you off your balance,
That, unworkable in itself,
Stops all the rest from working.
In fact, may you be dull —
If that is what a skilled,
Vigilant, flexible,
Unemphasised, enthralled
Catching of happiness is called.

Philip Larkin

We all wish a newly-born child (a "tightly folded bud") happiness in life — but what *is* happiness in life? Read the poem again now, feeling and thinking your way carefully into it, and see what different views on the matter you find there. What exactly is Philip Larkin's own feeling about it? What is there in the language of the poem that helps you to share in that feeling? With the help of these questions, say what you yourself feel about 'Born Yesterday' *as a poem*.

University of Cambridge, GCE 'O' Level English Literature (Plain Texts).

- Keep in mind what we have said about reading ("with the eye" and "with the ear") and note-making ("around the poem").
- Remember how we shaped notes into an essay pattern (section 5, 'Studying Single Poems'. p. 18).

Now, go through the process of reading, note-making and essay-writing for yourself *before* you compare your work with that of the student below. Elizabeth (who was 15 years old at the time) wrote her essay in about forty minutes. She had not seen the poem before.

Elizabeth's essay (uncorrected)

Our comments

"Born Yesterday" Philip Larkin

This is a joyful poem covering up a sad man. If you look at the poem superficially, without examining the thoughts behind it, it appears to be a simple, well thought out wish by a kind god parent for his newborn godchild, but to look at the poem deeper uncovers a man who appears to be sad and vulnerable, as well as confused.

He begins, slightly awed by the baby he is holding;
    "Tightly folded bud"
This is a beautiful line, conjuring up the image of a womb-creased 'scrunched-up' baby. It is tense and stiff in his hands like all new born babies are. The reference to a bud has two meanings to me. It is natural, and like a flower waiting to bloom the image of a bud promises a delightful change; a complete metamorphis.

The poet is cynical, making fun of other people who wish the baby beauty, innocence etc. He feels it is ironic that these people wish the baby the very things he feels are bound to make them unhappy. At the end of the first verse he says that if the things others wish her come true then:
    "Well, you're a lucky girl"

Larkin's poem invites us to think directly about the writer's feelings. Elizabeth sees this straight away — "This is a joyful poem covering up a sad man". In a simple statement she gets to what she sees as the heart of the poem.

She begins to show us *how* she gets to the heart of the poem.

She responds personally, not by simply saying "This is a beautiful line" but also by showing what it means *to her*, . . . what associations it has.

Does she get this right? Does Larkin think that she would be unlucky or unfortunate to have these traits — or, simply, that it is unlikely that it would prove possible? She doesn't clearly state what he *does* in fact wish for

But in the next verse he directly contradicts himself by saying that he would consider her unlucky or unfortunate to have these traits.

The whole poem centres around his attitude towards his fellows and his realization of the differences between "others" and himself. He honestly believes that true happiness stems from being completely and utterly ordinary and unnoticeable, almost invisible; the kind of person who is never noticed on the street and has no special features or talents.
"Nothing uncustomary to pull you off your balance."
To him life and happiness should be even, steady-balanced.

His idea of happiness is strange as well. He has designed, created, in the last four lines and ideal, perfect emotion. It is what he would *like* to feel. He thinks it is "skillful" and "vigilant". This implies it must be tended and nurtured if it is to survive; it is not a natural thing for him. It must be a constant suprise and cause 'joy anew' and it must allow freedom. But still he gets back to this overwhelming obsession of his:
"Unemphasised . . . happiness"
Perhaps he feels that if your joy is evident and apparent someone will endeavour to take it away from you.

This man is not happy. There is an underlying sadness within him that he expresses through his dry cynisism. Perhaps to express it directly would be to reveal too much of himself, to be vulnerable; unprotected. This poet has never been ordinary. He has always been different; a freak maybe even bullied or ostrecized(?) He would like to be ordinary. It could be his talent for poetry that has made him unhappy; it could be anything. We have no way of knowing. We are left with a sense of sadness, and of sympathy for Philip Larkin but it is touching — what he has written and felt for his godchild is a moving, sensitive insight into his inner thoughts. We feel honoured that he has allowed us to see into his head.

the child ("an average of talents") and the reasons why — i.e. excess in one direction makes life "unworkable" and "stops all the rest from working".
She perceives that the poem focusses every bit as much on Larkin as on the baby and that he values his difference from the norm while wishing the baby a balanced even dull existence. (There's an irony here, isn't there? — How far is *he* aware of it?) She is sensitive to the tone and voice of the poem.

A deeply thoughtful response to Larkin's view of happiness. She seeks out the implications of every word — "skilful", "vigilant" etc. . . . She is concerned, as poets are, with what particular words actually mean.

A thoughtful and justifiable speculation that goes beyond the poem but acknowledges that "we have no way of knowing" from the words on the page how true it may be.

Where Elizabeth might have said more:
She didn't really get to grips with the *language* of the poem though she felt its effects all right. We would have been interested to see something on the almost conversational tone: "not the usual stuff" . . . , "well, you're a lucky girl"; in fact, after the first three lines (with their rhyming "bud"/"would") everything is deliberately "non-poetic", in any flowery sense of the word. After the colon in line 3, Larkin's poetic skill, echoing the sense of the poem, goes into hiding. Everything becomes apparently flat and ordinary but the lines are given life by a careful use of stress and half-rhyme ("then"/"women"; "talents"/"balance"; "ordinary"/"uncustomary"). He uses a rhymed couplet at the end to close the poem formally.

The title is worth a second thought. The baby was "born yesterday" but when adults say 'I wasn't born yesterday' they mean they are not to be taken in. Does this relate to the poem?

Here are some examples of poetry questions from different examination boards for you to work on.

A   *From* University of Cambridge GCE 'O' Level English Literature (Plain Texts).

Read the following poem several times, and then answer the questions based on it.

The Jaguar

The apes yawn and adore their fleas in the sun.	1
The parrots shriek as if they were on fire, or strut	
Like cheap tarts to attract the stroller with the nut.	
Fatigued with indolence, tiger and lion	
Lie still as the sun. The boa-constrictor's coil	5
Is a fossil. Cage after cage seems empty, or	
Stinks of sleepers from the breathing straw.	
It might be painted on a nursery wall.	
But who runs like the rest past these arrives	9
At a cage where the crowd stands, stares, mesmerized,	
As a child at a dream, at a jaguar hurrying enraged	
Through prison darkness after the drills of his eyes	
On a short fierce fuse. Not in boredom —	13
The eye satisfied to be blind in fire,	
By the bang of blood in the brain deaf the ear —	
He spins from the bars, but there's no cage to him	
More than to the visionary his cell:	17
His stride is wildernesses of freedom:	
The world rolls under the long thrust of his heel.	
Over the cage floor the horizons come.	

Ted Hughes

42

Note: In line 9, 'who' means 'he who', or 'whoever'.
   In line 17, the word 'visionary' means a person who sees visions, perhaps prophetic, perhaps impossible: often the word refers to the religious mystic who chooses to live confined to a cell in order to give all his attention to visions of heaven.

(i) What is the general atmosphere of the zoo, and what response to their captivity do the various animals show (apart from the jaguar)? Do the parrots fit in with this 'general atmosphere'?
(ii) Say briefly what it is that seems to have attracted a 'crowd' to the jaguar rather than to the other animals. Why should the crowd stand 'mesmerized'?
(iii) From the middle of the third verse onwards the poem contains a succession of strange but striking phrases about the jaguar. Say as fully as you can what these phrases suggest to you about the jaguar and his captivity.
(iv) So far as time allows, write about anything in the poem — words, phrases, ideas, images, insights or anything else — that has especially struck you, or pleased you, or puzzled you, and that you have not included in what you have written already. Do you like the poem?

B *From* AEB GCE 'O' Level English Literature, Syllabus B

Either: (a) Read carefully the following poem, and then answer the questions based on it:

Anthem for Doomed Youth

What passing-bells for these who die as cattle?
   Only the monstrous anger of the guns.
   Only the stuttering rifles' rapid rattle
Can patter out their hasty orisons.
No mockeries for them from prayers or bells,
Nor any voice of mourning save the choirs,—
The shrill, demented choirs of wailing shells;
And bugles calling for them from sad shires.

What candles may be held to speed them all?
   Not in the hands of boys, but in their eyes
   Shall shine the holy glimmers of goodbyes.
The pallor of girls' brows shall be their pall;
Their flowers the tenderness of silent minds,
And each slow dusk a drawing-down of blinds.

Wilfred Owen (1893–1918)

(i) What is the poet's attitude to war and how is it shown?   (6 marks)
(ii) Examine the way in which the poet deals with sound in the poem.
                                                                (6 marks)
(iii) In an earlier version of the poem lines 1, 3 and 7 had been, respectively:

"What passing-bells for you who die in herds"

"Only the stuttering rifles' rattled words"
"And long-drawn sighs of wailing shells"

Examine the changes in **two** of the lines and say what has been gained or lost by them. (4 marks)

(iv) State in your own words how the "doomed youth" will be honoured
(4 marks)

Or: (b) Read carefully the following poem, then answer the questions based on it:

The Pond

With nets and kitchen sieves they raid the pond,
Chasing the minnows into bursts of mud,
Scooping and chopping, raking up frond after frond
Of swollen weed after a week of flood.   4

Thirty or forty minnows bob and flash
In every jam-jar hoarded on the edge,
While the shrill children with each ill-aimed splash
Haul out another dozen as they dredge.   8

Choked to its banks, the pond spills out its store
Of frantic life. Nothing can drain it dry
Of what it breeds: it breeds so effortlessly
Theft seems to leave it richer than before.   12

The nostrils snuff its rank bouquet — how warm,
How lavish, foul, and indiscriminate, fat
With insolent appetite and thirst, so that
The stomach almost heaves to see it swarm.   16

But trapped in glass the minnows flail and fall,
Sink, with upended bellies showing white,
After an hour I look and see that all
But four or five have died. The greenish light   20

Ripples to stillness, while the children bend
To spoon the corpses out, matter-of-fact,
Absorbed: as if creation's prodigal act
Shrank to this empty jam-jar in the end.   24

Anthony Thwaite, born 1930

(i)   What qualities in the children does the poem convey? How is the effect achieved? (6 marks)

(ii) How is the notion of "frantic life" (line 10) reinforced in the poem?
(6 marks)

(iii) Explain what the poet means when he says:
      "as if creation's prodigal act
      Shrank to this empty jam-jar in the end"
                  (lines 23—24)

(4 marks)

(iv) Comment on the effectiveness of **two** of the following expressions:
        bursts of mud (line 2)
        rank bouquet (line 13)
        flail and fall (line 17)

(4 marks)

C *From* SREB CSE English Literature, Syllabus R

Read the following poem carefully before answering *both* questions.

Ambulances

Closed like confessionals, they thread
Loud noons of cities, giving back
None of the glances they absorb.
Light glossy grey, arms on a plaque,
They come to rest at any kerb:
All streets in time are visited.

Then children strewn on steps or road,
Or women coming from the shops
Past smells of different dinners, see
A wildwhite face that overtops
Red stretcher-blankets momently
As it is carried in and stowed,

And sense the solving emptiness
That lies just under all we do,
And for a second get it whole
So permanent and blank and true.
The fastened doors recede. "Poor soul,"
They whisper at their own distress;

For borne away in deadened air
May go the sudden shout of loss
Round something nearly at an end,
And what cohered in it across
The years, the unique random blend
Of families and fashions, there

At last begins to loosen. Far
From the exchange of love to lie
Unreachable inside a room
The traffic parts to let go by
Brings closer what is left to come,
And dulls to distance all we are.

Philip Larkin

1 Select three phrases from the poem which strike you as particularly effective, or which simply appeal to you and explain, in each case, what it was about the phrase that made you select it. (3 marks)

45

2 Write about the poem as a whole in any way you like. Possible starting points could be: an expansion of the ideas in the poem, or an examination of the language and style used by Philip Larkin — taking care not to overlap any answer to question 1 — but these are suggestions only, and should not put you off any other idea or approach you may have. Your answer, however, should be in continuous writing. (7 marks)

D *From* AEB GCE 'A' Level English, Alternative Syllabus

Read the following passage:

One summer evening (led by her)* I found   * Nature
A little boat tied to a willow tree
Within a rocky cave, its usual home.
Straight I unloosed her chain, and stepping in
Pushed from the shore. It was an act of stealth
And troubled pleasure, nor without the voice
Of mountain-echoes did my boat move on;
Leaving behind her still, on either side,
Small circles glittering idly in the moon,
Until they melted all into one track
Of sparkling light. But now, like one who rows,
Proud of his skill, to reach a chosen point
With an unswerving line, I fixed my view
Upon the summit of a craggy ridge,
The horizon's utmost boundary; far above
Was nothing but the stars and the grey sky.
She was an elfin pinnace;† lustily   † a small boat
I dipped my oars into the silent lake,
And, as I rose upon the stroke, my boat
Went heaving through the water like a swan;
When, from behind that craggy steep till then
The horizon's bound, a huge peak, black and huge,
As if with voluntary power instinct
Upreared its head. I struck and struck again,
And growing still in stature the grim shape
Towered up between me and the stars, and still,
For so it seemed, with purpose of its own
And measured motion like a living thing,
Strode after me. With trembling oars I turned,
And through the silent water stole my way
Back to the covert of the willow tree;
There in her mooring-place I left my bark,
And through the meadows homeward went, in grave
And serious mood; but after I had seen
That spectacle, for many days, my brain
Worked with a dim and undetermined sense
Of unknown modes of being; o'er my thoughts
There hung a darkness, call it solitude

Or blank desertion. No familiar shapes
Remained, no pleasant images of trees,
Of sea or sky, no colours of green fields;
But huge and mighty forms, that do not live
Like living men, moved slowly through the mind
By day, and were a trouble to my dreams.

Wordsworth is here describing an adventure he had during his childhood. Examine the passage carefully, tracing the feelings which the author conveys to us and pointing out some of the ways in which his techniques of writing make those feelings and the atmosphere clear to the reader. You should consider such things as tone, rhythm, vocabulary and imagery.

(40 marks)

Checklist

Dos

- Do read the poem several times both with the eye and the ear — even if you have to mouth it quietly to yourself in order to hear it aloud.
- Do use writing (i.e. jottings) to help you develop your thoughts. Few people can hold all the details of what they want to say in their heads and write an essay straight off without notes.
- Do give the poet the benefit of any doubts you may have until you have really got to grips with his or her poem. It's very rare for examiners to set trivial poems.
- Do be positive and look for the 'plus' points as well as any criticisms you may have.
- Do tolerate puzzling bits. You don't have to be able to paraphrase everything — some lines may remain elusive.
- Do comment fully on particular lines that appeal to you — you'll write best about the parts of the poem that you like.

Don'ts

- Don't fake a response i.e. by telling the examiner what you *think* he wants to hear rather than what you really think and feel yourself.
- Don't be afraid to use the first person when it feels appropriate.
- Don't assume that you have to be either 'for' or 'against' a poem. If you dislike the poem you're probably best advised to avoid the question; there's little purpose in listing a lot of negative points.
- Don't quote lines or phrases simply to let them speak for themselves. Make them work for their place in your essay.
- Don't simply say that you like a line or phrase or that "it's beautiful" and leave it at that. Say why.
- Don't assume the poem has to have a hidden meaning, that it's a mystery you have to solve. When you have read "with eye and ear" and thought around the poem, trust your judgement.

List of poems quoted in the text

Anonymous	Shantytown
William Blake	The Sick Rose
Charles Causley	Mary, Mary Magdalene
Robert Frost	Nothing Gold Can Stay
	Spring Pools
Thomas Hardy	Men Who March Away
Ted Hughes	Esther's Tomcat
	The Jaguar
	The Warm and the Cold
Philip Larkin	Ambulances
	Born Yesterday
Liz Lochhead	Why I Gave You the Chinese Plate
Don Marquis	The Tom-cat
Gerda Mayer	Poplar
Grace Nichols	The Fat Black Woman Goes Shopping
Wilfred Owen	Anthem for Doomed Youth
	The Send-off
Sylvia Plath	Metaphors
	Mirror
Ezra Pound	In a Station of the Metro
Colin Rowbotham	Dissection
Edward Thomas	Cock-Crow
Anthony Thwaite	The Pond
William Carlos Williams	A Negro Woman
William Wordsworth	"One summer evening . . . " from The Prelude

Arthur Meighen High School